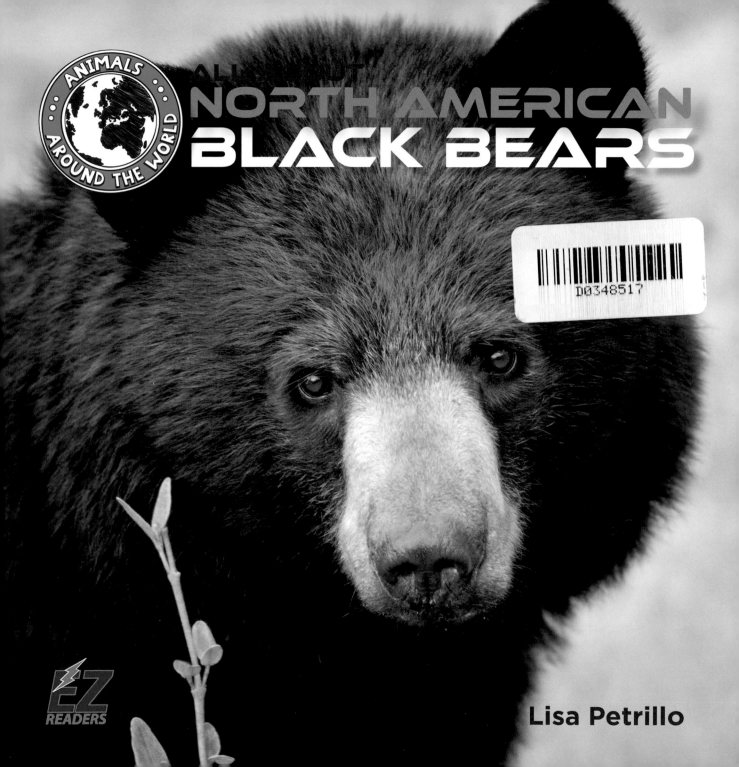

ANIMALS AROUND THE WORLD

ALL ABOUT
# NORTH AMERICAN
# BLACK BEARS

EZ READERS

Lisa Petrillo

## Creating Young Nonfiction Readers

*EZ Readers* lets children delve into nonfiction at beginning reading levels. Young readers are introduced to new concepts, facts, ideas, and vocabulary.

## Tips for Reading Nonfiction with Beginning Readers

### Talk about Nonfiction
Begin by explaining that nonfiction books give us information that is true. The book will be organized around a specific topic or idea, and we may learn new facts through reading.

### Look at the Parts
Most nonfiction books have helpful features. Our *EZ Readers* include a Contents page, an index, and color photographs. Share the purpose of these features with your reader.

### Contents
Located at the front of a book, the Contents displays a list of the big ideas within the book and where to find them.

### Index
An index is an alphabetical list of topics and the page numbers where they are found.

### Glossary
Located at the back of the book, a glossary contains key words/phrases that are related to the topic.

### Photos/Charts
A lot of information can be found by "reading" the charts and photos found within nonfiction text. Help your reader learn more about the different ways information can be displayed.

With a little help and guidance about reading nonfiction, you can feel good about introducing a young reader to the world of *EZ Readers* nonfiction books.

## Mitchell Lane
### PUBLISHERS

2001 SW 31st Avenue
Hallandale, FL 33009
www.mitchelllane.com

First Edition, 2020.

Author: Lisa Petrillo
Designer: Ed Morgan
Editor: Sharon F. Doorasamy

Names/credits:
Title: All About North American Black Bears / by Lisa Petrillo
Description: Hallandale, FL : Mitchell Lane Publishers, [2020]

Series: Animals Around the World

Library bound ISBN: 9781680204179

eBook ISBN: 9781680204186

EZ readers is an imprint of Mitchell Lane Publishers

Photo credits: Freepik.com, Shutterstock.com, p. 14-15 DieterMeryl Getty Images, p. 16-17 Keith Levit / Design Pics Getty Images, mapchart.net

# CONTENTS

Black Bears 4

Where Do Black Bears Live? 22

Interesting Facts 23

Parts of a Bear 23

Glossary 24

Further Reading 24

On the Internet 24

Index 24

Black bears live in wooded mountains, forests, and swamps. They come in many colors. Some are black. Others are brown and even white.

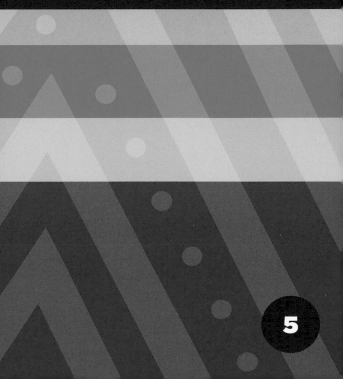

Bears can run as fast as a car. They stand to see and smell better. They grow as tall as a six-foot man. They are chubby as a barrel.

American black bears look cuddly. But they can be fierce. Their claws are sharp as knives. They use their claws to climb trees.

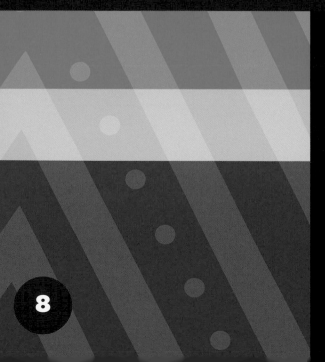

Black bears eat a lot. They love berries, honey, and small animals.

Male bears are **boars**. Boars tend to be loners. Female bears are **sows**. Baby bears are **cubs**. Cubs stay with their mothers for about three years.

Mother bears dig **dens**. Cubs are born in dens. Inside the dens, cubs wrestle with each other to stay warm. They can't open their eyes for weeks.

Bears sleep through the winter. Mother bears wake up only to feed their cubs.

After their long winter sleep, a mother bear brings her cubs out of the den. She protects them. Hungry wolves and other bears kill cubs. People hunt bears.

Black bears are great swimmers, diggers, and catchers of fish. They live for about 25 years in the wild.

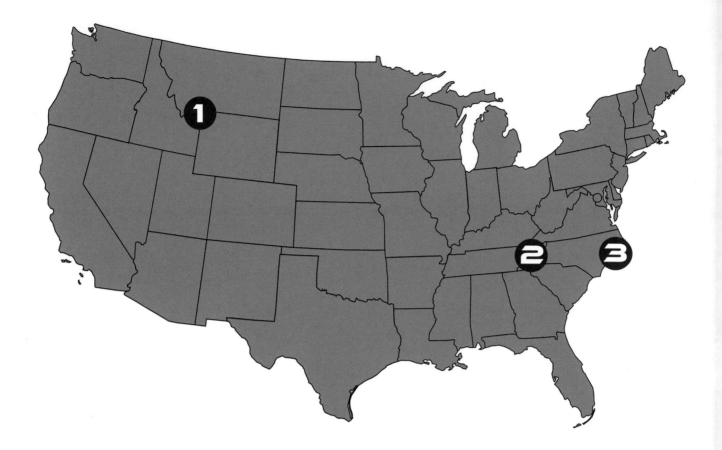

## WHERE DO BEARS LIVE?

Here are three National Parks where you can see them:

1. Yellowstone National Park in Wyoming, Montana, and Idaho

2. The Great Smoky Mountains in North Carolina and Tennessee

3. Alligator River National Wildlife Refuge in North Carolina

# INTERESTING FACTS

- Bears communicate with growls, grunts, and moans.

- Bear teeth are sharp, with pointed front teeth good for biting. Their back teeth are flatter for crushing and grinding plants and nuts.

- Bears keep their noses wet to sharpen their sense of smell.

- Bears carried great importance with Native American people.

# PARTS OF A BEAR

**Paws**
Black bears have front paws that are five inches long.

**Eyes**
Black bears have sharp night vision.

**Short legs**
Bears have short, thick limbs that carry a heavy body, and a big head.

**Tails**
Bears have stubby tails five inches long.

**Claws**
Black bear claws are more than an inch long.

# GLOSSARY

**boar**
Male bear

**cub**
A baby bear

**den**
A bear's home or resting place

**sow**
Female bear

# FURTHER READING

Carney, Elizabeth. *Bears*. Washington, DC: National Geographic Books, 2016.

Markle, Sandra. *Growing Up Wild: Bears*. New York, NY: Atheneum Books for Young Readers, 2000.

Swinburne, Stephen R. *Black Bear: North America's Bear*. Honesdale, PA: Boyds Mills Press, 2003.

# ON THE INTERNET

**National Geographic: American Black Bear**
https://www.nationalgeographic.com/animals/
mammals/a/american-black-bear/

**Native American Bear Mythology**
http://www.native-languages.org/legends-bear.htm

# INDEX

| | |
|---|---|
| Boars | 12 |
| Cubs | 12 |
| Forests | 5 |
| Mountains | 5 |
| Native American | 23 |
| Sows | 12 |
| Swamps | 5 |